FIFTY FAST FACTS ABOUT THE AMERICAN REVOLUTION

MIDDLE GRADE GUIDE

CONTENTS

PART I

The Role of Economics
In the American Revolution

10 Fast Facts

ECONOMICS

It's been said that money is the root of all evil. It certainly was at the root of the War of Independence. While the true cost of the American Revolution goes far beyond money - including lives, family relations, businesses, and global reputations - debt, taxation, and financial control were certainly at the heart of the struggle for independence from England. Read on to discover 10 fast facts about the American economy that led to the Revolutionary War.

1

WORLD WAR WOUNDS THE WALLET

Twenty years before American colonists fought against the British army, they fought alongside them during the Seven Years War. Fought between 1756 and 1763, many historians call this war the first global conflict, as empires fought across the continents to expand their territories and demonstrate their dominance. Britain and France were the major combatants, and the two nations battled their way across parts of Europe, Asia, and North America. Britain may have emerged victorious, but heavily in debt. Dutch and British bankers had lent the British government so much money that, by the end of the war, the national debt had doubled. Desperate to repay their creditors, both King George III and the British parliament argued that since its colonies benefited by securing its borders, they should contribute to paying off the war debt. Not only that, but England also sent permanent regiments of 10,000 soldiers to the American colonies to prevent future attacks. Of course, this required even more funding. The solution? A series of taxes, tariffs, duties and fines imposed on the American colonies to cover the military and naval expenses. The problem? The colonists had no say in what was taxed, how much they were charged, or how the funds were spent. Known as 'taxation without representation', it would be the rallying cry of the separatists for years to come.

2

BRITISH LAWS WERE BAD FOR BUSINESS

At least, they were bad for American businesses. The practice of mercantilism brought enormous wealth to Britain in the 1600 and 1700s. Mercantilism is an economic policy that enables a country to generate much of its wealth through exports. For Britain, this meant that they would supply themselves with cheap raw materials from its colonies - like wood, cotton, and sugar - then transform these into expensive finished goods like ships, fabric and rum which they could sell back to the colonists at a higher price and with import taxes. For the colonies, it meant that there were rules for what items they could make or grow, who they could make it for, and what price they could sell it. Even worse, mercantilism emphasized profits above all else, leading to colonial inflation, taxation, and legalized slavery. In the Americas, colonies owned by the Netherlands, Spain, and France neighboured the 13 colonies, but British law prohibited trade with anyone other than England's own merchants. Smuggling rings soon sprang up, making fortunes for colonists like Samuel Adams willing to ignore British trade law. As the Seven Years' War ended, Britain tightened its control over colonial trade to repay its war debt, but the American economy soon suffered as it forced colonial businesses to pay higher prices, limited to British approved inventory only, and paying British imposed taxes.

TAXES WENT FROM SWEET TO SOUR

D eeply in debt from the Seven Years' War, Britain's economic dominance was in decline by the 1760s. Losing revenue to colonial smugglers, as well as mounting opposition to mercantile regulations and the human rights abuses of the slave trade, had all taken their toll on the British economy. Parliament took swift action to rebalance the books. Taxation seemed the quickest and most effective way to regain prosperity and refill British bank accounts. First came the Sugar Act of 1764. Introduced by prime minister George Grenville, the Sugar Act, also known as the Plantation Act, aimed to achieve three goals at once. First, it tightened punishments on smuggling. Next, it raised tariffs on sugar produced anywhere other than a British colony. Finally, it gave a near monopoly on the sugar trade to British-owned plantations and merchants. On the surface, the Sugar Act looked like a win for everyone. In reality, however, the tightened regulations allowed British customs commissions to seize and confiscate valuable cargo and transport it all the way to the northern colony of Nova Scotia for processing under the authority of the British Vice-Admiralty Court. It wasn't just prohibited goods they took. Officials could seize any cargo they considered suspect. If shipmasters and merchants wanted their cargo back, it was several days' journey by sea, followed by a trial to prove their innocence, all at their own expense. Colonists were furious, believing that the new taxes, the seizure of their goods, and these non-jury trials violated their rights as British citizens.

BUT IT DIDN'T STOP THERE. The following year, Parliament introduced The Stamp Act. This was a common form of taxation in England, requiring certain documents like newspapers, pamphlets, and printed paper materials to be marked with an official stamp. That same year, 1765, yet another tax, The Quartering Act. This time, colonists didn't pay the tax with money, instead they were required to provide housing, supplies, and transportation to the British military whenever it was required. The British Parliament argued these taxes benefited the colonies, and provided them with the very sweet deal of naval and military protection for a minimal price. To colonists, these taxes were decidedly sour.

4

TAXES WERE NOT THEIR CUP OF TEA

Although the colonists were angry about these new taxes, their protests were mostly nonviolent, choosing to fight economic problems with economic solutions. In 1765, nine colonies sent representatives to New York to convene the Stamp Act Congress and organize a systematic boycott of British-made and imported goods. Simply put, to avoid paying taxes, Americans refused to buy items that included a tax. The boycott worked. In 1766, just two years after issuing the Sugar and Stamp Acts, English merchants had lost nearly all of their customers in the colonies and pressured the British Parliament to repeal the taxes. As the boycotts continued into 1770, nearly all of its new taxes except for one, the tax on tea. The tea tax remained relatively unchanged in the colonies for nearly a decade. Like sugar, colonists often bought tea smuggled in through Dutch traders to avoid the tax, but unlike sugar, the tea tax had been relatively unenforced. Then, in 1773, following a shuffle in the British Parliament and an overproduction of over 17,000,000 pounds of tea by the British owned East India Company, parliament once again turned its attention to the money-making potential of taxing the colonies. In a power play by the new parliament to reassert its right to tax its colonies directly, as well as generate profit for the financially troubled shipping company, they issued a new and restrictive Tea Tax. It was a serious miscalculation, and, in the eyes of the colonists, it was an act of taxation tyranny that they simply could not allow. As with the boycott of 1765, the colonists decided peaceful protest was the best method to combat these taxation tyrants. Rather than resorting to violence, the colonists threw a party. A Boston Tea Party.

5

TAXATION WITHOUT REPRESENTATION

In 1765, twenty-seven representatives from nine American colonies sent three documents by ship to England. These documents outlined their opposition to the new taxes and tariffs on the colonies, arguing Britain had violated its own laws by imposing taxation without representation. Simply put, England and its colonies operated under the legal principle that residents could only be taxed if they had a representative in government who could vote for or against any new tax laws. This rule dated back over 500 years, when in 1215 English barons forced King John to sign the Magna Carta, the Great Charter declaring the king had no power to tax citizens not represented in parliament. In response, Britain argued some colonies had official agents who travelled to London to share colonial issues and grievances. Benjamin Franklin, for example, was the official agent of Pennsylvania, but colonists were quick to point out he was not a member of the British parliament and could not vote. Unwilling to concede the legal argument or allow a colonist to join the prestigious ranks of parliament, the British government instead issued the Declaratory Act. This new law stated Britain had the right to tax its colonies however it wished. This was a serious miscalculation by the British politicians and viewed as an act of tyranny by the colonists.

Up to this point, the colonists had always stressed their loyalty to the monarchy in their complaints, asking simply that they should have the same rights and protections as British citizens in England. By the late 1760s, however, the constant seizure of their goods, the denial of jury trials for trade offences, imposing taxation without representation, and, finally, the Declaratory Act, left colonists wondering if the British monarchy was still loyal to them.

AMERICANS WERE BETTER OFF THAN THE BRITISH

E ven with the imposition of new taxes, the combination of cheap land and seemingly endless natural resources meant that by 1774 American colonists averaged the highest annual income in the western world at £13.85. In Britain, the average per capita income was between £10-12, and even less in France. According to the historian Alice Hansen Jones, the average free white male earned approximately £16 per year, while indentured servants (those who signed a contract agreeing to work for a set number of years) received food, shelter, clothing, and a small wage equal to roughly £9 per year. These amounts varied by region. The South was the richest region, with an average income of £18 per year for free white men, while New Englanders averaged £12 per year, the least among the colonies but still higher than the average incomes in either England or France. The prospect of going to war was a threat to one of the highest living standards in the world, with no guarantee of success and the possibility of losing their property and incomes entirely.

OF COURSE, this wealth was not evenly distributed. Enslaved persons in the colonies were rarely paid a wage, if ever, and were forced to endure hard labour and poor living conditions without legal protection or recourse. The First Nations tribes, who numbered in the hundreds of thousands, were not included in the consideration of wealth distribution and had little access to the colonial economy. And while women shaped the consumer market, dictating the kinds of items sold in shops or brought to market by local farms as they were the dominant purchaser of household goods, the right of a woman to own property, possess an income, or operate a business was strictly controlled, if not completely denied, until laws permitting white women access to financial structures began to appear in the late 1770s. Women of colour were denied similar rights for more than a century afterward.

MERCHANTS DIDN'T WANT WAR

A lthough business in the colonies relied on entrepreneurs, the desire to run your own business didn't mean American merchants wanted to run their own economy - or fight a war over it. Wars disrupted trade, bankrupted governments, and scared away customers. Back in England, British merchants also feared a war with America would be bad for business. A 1775 petition from the merchants, traders, manufacturers and other citizens of the city of Bristol to King George III urged "that none can profit by the continuance of this war". In Bristol they relied on the importation of American wheat, importing "no less than one million bushels" while the colonists relied on the supply of goods not only from Britain but also its network of colonies worldwide. Meanwhile, the Continental colonies were still recovering from a recessionary slump in the 1760s, British currency was in short supply, and many worried that renewed hostilities between the Americans and Britain would ruin trade entirely. In 1775 the British Parliament received another petition, this one from the Merchants, Traders, and Others of the City of London, who urged the House of Commons to reconsider the taxation on the American colonists, arguing that taxation was impossible as "from Rhode-Island northwards they have no money; that their trade is generally carried on by barter" and that Parliament "might almost as soon have raised the dead as one hundred Pounds from any individual in the Province of the Massachusetts Bay", meaning it would be easier to raise the dead than to raise money for taxes in the colonies.

SOMETIMES WAR IS GOOD FOR BUSINESS

C lothing, arming, and feeding 12,000 soldiers takes a lot of material, ammunition, and food. In Britain, merchants and artisans vied for lucrative contracts with the Crown to become official suppliers. It wasn't so easy for the Continental Army, who struggled with a lack of funding and materials. Even with these challenges, enterprising entrepreneurs found lucrative ways to support the cause of liberty while making a tidy profit for themselves. German baker Christopher Ludwick (sometimes spelled Ludwig) first arrived in Philadelphia in 1753, having already been a soldier for the Austrian and Prussian armies and serving as a baker aboard the British Navy. He opened a wildly successful bakery, introducing gingerbread and other confections to the colonies. When the revolutionary war broke out, Ludwick stayed loyal to the Americans who had supported him and his business. When George Washington wrote to Congress desperate for supplies and funds for the winter at Valley Forge, Christopher Ludwick donated his services and refused to take a salary, instead promising to bake 135 loaves of bread for every 100 pounds of flour he received. Ludwick was true to his word, and stayed on as Director of Baking for another five years, proving himself invaluable not only for his baking talents but also his ability to speak German to captured Hessian mercenaries and his first-hand knowledge of the British Navy. Although he took no direct payment from Washington, his management, flour shipments, and transportation earned Ludwick valuable credit and commissions. He frequently dined with the Washingtons, who served dinner guests samples of Ludwick's cookies and pastries. Soon, they commissioned Ludwick for their own celebrations. At the end of the war, Ludwick had amassed a small personal fortune. Years later Napoleon would remark that an "army marches on its stomach." As for the Continental Army, Ludwick filled their stomachs with fresh cookies and bread. Today visitors can still see the field ovens and cookie cutters Ludwick and his bakers used on display at Valley Forge.

BEFORE THE DOLLAR, THERE WAS THE CONTINENTAL

While John Hancock's name is the largest on the Declaration of Independence, it was the signature beside it, much smaller and crammed off to the right, that would sign off on the bills that largely paid for the Revolution. By 1780, five years into the war, the colonial economy was nearly bankrupt and the paper currency, called Continentals, was next to worthless because of mounting inflation and a stalled income. Enter Robert Morris, the self-made global entrepreneur with a big appetite and deep pockets. While he had originally opposed independence as being bad for business, ultimately Morris stood with the Pennsylvania delegation and signed his name to the Declaration. With his international trade network and European connections, Morris became the Superintendent of Finance, the position predating the Treasury Secretary. Morris put up his considerable personal credit to fund supplies and secure loans from friendly foreign countries eager to undermine Britain's economic stronghold. Promissory notes, called "Morris Notes" circulated among the ranks of the army in place of paper currency, while Morris used his merchant ships to smuggle in European supplies of guns and gunpowder. For three years Morris bankrolled the supplies of the Continental army on his own, signing his name to bills for cattle from Connecticut, flour from Virginia, and weapons shipped in through the Caribbean and substituting his personal line of credit for the devalued Continental currency.

VICTORY COMES AT A PRICE

Before Robert Morris stepped in to fund the Revolutionary War in 1780, the United States Congress issued over 400 million in colonial paper money to pay the escalating price of the war. Printing its own currency, called Continentals, plus the inevitable interruption to the economy caused by the war, resulted in mounting inflation. Food riots broke out as prices rose rapidly, ongoing battles destroyed property and infrastructure, and, to further sabotage the war effort, the British government hired skilled counterfeiters to flood the American market with fake currency and further devalue American paper money. By the end of the war, the new nation had spent more than $150 million. Creditors included the nations of France and Spain, as well as individual financiers like Robert Morris and Haym Salomon. The states argued over how best to resolve their debt until the 1790s when Congress approved Treasury Secretary Alexander Hamilton's proposal of the First Bank of the United States to cover the cost of war debts and establish national credit for global markets.

QUIZ ONE

Economics

TEST YOUR KNOWLEDGE

Now that you've learned 10 Fast Facts about the Economy during the American Revolution, here's a quick quiz to test your knowledge.

Question One:
What was the war fought between 1756 and 1763 called:
a) The Dutch-English War
b) The Hundred Years War
c) The Continental War
d) The Seven Years War

Answer: D, The Seven Years War

Question Two:
The economic policy enabling a country to generate much of its wealth through exports is called:
a) Supply and Demand
b) Mercantilism
c) Capitalism
d) Free Trade

Answer: B, Mercantilism

Question Three:
To reclaim goods wrongfully seized under the Sugar Act, merchants had to attend court in which Northern colony:
a) Connecticut
b) Newfoundland
c) Nova Scotia
d) Rhode Island

Answer: C, Nova Scotia

Question Four:
How did colonists avoid paying taxes between 1765 and 1773:
a) They bought smuggled goods
b) The boycotted taxable items
c) They used nonviolent protests
d) All of the above

Answer: D, All of the above

Question Five:
Which British law declared the king had no power to tax citizens not represented in parliament.:
a) The Stamp Act
b) The Plantation Act
c) The Magna Carta
d) The Royal Proclamation

Answer: C, The Magna Carta

Question Six:
Which region was home to the richest American colonies:
a) The South
b) The North

c) New England

d) New York

Answer: A, The South

Question Seven:

In 1775 the British Parliament received a petition from London merchants suggesting it would be easier to raise the dead than to do what:

a) Raise an objection

b) Raise a little hell

c) Raise up one's voice

d) Raise taxes in the colonies

Answer: D, Raise taxes in the colonies

Question Eight:

Besides providing bread for the troops, what other skill did colonist Christopher Ludwick have:

a) He spoke German to captured Hessian prisoners

b) He spoke fluent French with Lafayette

c) He spoke several First Nations languages

d) He was deaf but could read lips

Answer: A, He spoke German to captured Hessian prisoners

Question Nine:

Which of the following did NOT devalue the Continental currency:

a) Inflation

b) British counterfeiting

c) Minting coins

d) Bankruptcy

Answer: C, Minting coins

Question Ten:

At the end of the Revolutionary War, how much had the nation spent in dollar equivalent?

a) 400 million

b) 150 million

c) 1 million

d) 1 billion

Answer: B, 150 million dollars

PARAGRAPH WRITING: ECONOMICS

Using the facts we found on the previous pages, we'll use the 8x8 model to create a sample paragraph. As you read the paragraph, see if you can spot the foolproof formula for paragraph writing. It goes like this:

Topic Sentence (TS)
    To begin with
    For Example
    Next
    Additionally
    This clearly shows
    Finally
    Closing Sentence (CS) and Concluding Phrase (CP)

There are several concluding phrases that you can choose from. Try one of these instead of using "in conclusion…"

- Overall
- All in all
- Clearly

- Even though
- Having considered all of the facts
- Thus

Following is an example question of a question prompt and a sample paragraph response. At the end of the sample paragraph, we'll give you a few other prompts to use for practicing your own paragraphs.

Question Prompt: *Which economic factor was the most important leading up to the American Revolution?*

Although there were many economic factors leading up to the American Revolution, the most important one was taxation. To begin with, Britain began imposing a series of new taxes on the North American colonies to cover the cost of the Seven Years' War. For example, Britain posted permanent regiments of 10,000 soldiers across the Americas and demanded the colonists be the ones to pay for this protection through new tariffs on imported goods. Next, Britain imposed a new series of taxes including the Sugar Act of 1764 and the Stamp Act of 1765 that angered the colonists so much they boycotted buying these items. Once Britain realized they weren't earning taxes on the boycotted items, it imposed the Quartering Act requiring colonists to provide housing, supplies, and transportation to the British military instead of paying money through taxation. This clearly shows Britain was determined to have the colonists pay taxes, even if they paid in goods and services instead of currency. Finally, the British parliament refused to acknowledge that the colonists were enduring taxation without representation, which was illegal according to Britain's own laws, and would not allow the colonies to have their own representatives in parliament to vote for or against new laws. Clearly Britain's insistence to impose taxes which the colonists felt were unjust was the most important economic factor leading to war.

Try it for yourself - Write an 8x8 paragraph using the facts you found in the first 10 chapters. Answer one of the following prompts:

1. What examples of taxation without representation took place in the American colonies?
2. Describe the economy of the American colonies leading up to and during the war?
3. Explain the economic reasons colonists had for and against the Revolutionary War?

PART II

The Players

10 Fast Facts

THE PLAYERS

While the War of Independence was fought between the American colonists and the British forces, they weren't the only groups taking part in the conflict. From German mercenaries to the French Navy to First Nations warriors, there were a number of players in the great game of strategy, stealth, and strength that would determine who would ultimately control the destiny of a continent.

THERE WAS A LOT OF NAME CALLING

It's impossible to know who's who during the American Revolution without a lot of name calling. From teachers to textbook writers, as well as historians and the heroes themselves, all use a variety of names when referring to who fought who during the Revolution. While war is a very serious business, both sides of the conflict used a number of nicknames and some not-so-nice names to describe the combatants. Frequently, the Continental Army is referred to as 'Minutemen', 'Patriots', and 'Washington's Army' in deference to their military commander-in-chief, George Washington. Meanwhile, historians interchangeably use the terms 'Regulars', 'The Crown', 'The British', 'The English' or even 'Redcoats' to describe British land forces, but the colonists were more likely to use derogatory names like 'devils', 'lobster-backs', 'bloody backs', or the alliterative 'Bloody British'.

THE NEW CONTINENTAL ARMY LOOKED A LOT LIKE THE OLD CONTINENTAL ARMY

The men who fought for America were called the Continental Army. Prior to the Revolutionary War, however, whenever Britain referred to 'The Continent', it generally meant Continental Europe. In many ways, this new, American Continental Army functioned a lot like the previous continental armies of Europe. It had the same ranking systems for soldiers and officers, followed the same customs and rules of engagement, and even included soldiers from European countries. While largely made up of men from the Thirteen Colonies, both American-born and immigrants, as well as freemen, enslaved persons, and some First Nations warriors, the Continental Army had international support. Spain sent weapons and currency to help fight against its old foe, England. When the war began, France initially sent only supplies. Soon, however, they were sending French troops and the French Navy.

13

THE BRITISH ARMY WEREN'T ROYAL

Officially, British forces were first sent to keep the peace, enforce the law, and maintain control over the Thirteen American Colonies. While Britain referred to its seafaring force as the Royal Navy, the land forces of the Army did not all share in the title 'Royal'. Why not?

THE PREFIX 'ROYAL' was only given to certain army corps or regiments that had once received the title as a battle honour from the ruling king or queen during a previous war. English tradition dictated that armies were historically under the direct control of English lords and nobles, not the king or queen. These nobles paid for and commanded their own forces until obliged to serve the monarch in times of war, although the nobles themselves rarely fought. During the Revolutionary War, many regiments that had been awarded the use of the prefix 'Royal' in previous wars were again deployed on behalf of the king, including the 1st Regiment (Royal Regiment of Foot), the 7th Regiment (Royal Fusiliers) and the 42nd Regiment (Royal Highlanders) among many others. So what makes the Royal Navy so royal? That name dates back to the Middle Ages when

England's King Alfred created the Royal Navy as a vast but single force to fight off Viking invaders. The navy was directly under the king's command, much like the modern American president who is considered the Commander-in-Chief of the American military, thus making it the Royal Navy.

14

HESSIANS WERE HIRED HENCHMEN

For a century prior to the American War of Independence, the German state of Hesse-Cassel had a powerful reputation based on its skillful military training and the mandatory military service of its young men. The state of Hesse-Cassel earned a huge income by lending these trained soldiers to Britain to subsidize its own fighting forces overseas. When the American Revolution began, Britain once again hired Hessian troops to fight alongside the British Army. Sometimes referred to as 'mercenaries,' 'soldiers-for-hire,' or 'hired guns' Hessian soldiers fought at every major battle during the Revolution. Remarkably, although they fought for the British, after the War thousands of Hessians decided to remain in the United States and ultimately became American citizens.

THE FRIENDLY FRENCH FOUGHT FEROCIOUSLY

L afayette might be the most famous of the fighting French soldiers of the war, but several of his countrymen fought alongside the Continental army to defeat their old foe, England. Previously, French and British forces had fought in North America before the American Revolution over their territorial rights and borders. Known as the French and Indian War, the conflict began in 1754 as the European imperial conflict between Britain and France, known as the Seven Years' War, stretched across the Atlantic Ocean and into the colonies of North America. The Treaty of Paris ended both wars in 1763, with France losing significant colonial holdings, including the Canadian territories, Quebec, the Great Lakes Basin, and the east bank of the Mississippi River. So when the American colonists took up arms against Britain and King George III, the French king enthusiastically pledged his support against his old foe. Along with 12,000 soldiers and nearly 32,000 sailors, France sent food, supplies, and weapons to assist the Americans. While the Marquis du Lafayette remains the most famous French soldier of the American Revolution, General Jean-Baptiste Donatien de Vimeur, comte de Rochambeau and Admiral François Joseph Paul de Grasse were integral to the success of the Continental Army.

16

THE WAR DIVIDED THE FIRST NATIONS

The First Nations, sometimes referred to as Native Americans, were divided in their support during the Revolutionary War. When the colonial militia laid siege to Boston in 1775, First Nations near Stockbridge, Massachusetts showed their support by sending 17 men to fight on behalf of the colonial militia. Other groups resisted the American colonists and formed an alliance with Canadian settlers and British Forces, defeating an American invasion into Canada in 1775. For some groups, the war caused internal division. The Cherokee nation split between support of the colonists and the British Army. In the territory now known as New York State and the Canadian provinces of Ontario and Quebec the Iroquois Confederacy, a powerful alliance of six Native American nations was similarly divided. Two nations, the Oneida and Tuscarora, sided with American colonists while the remaining four, including the exceptional fighting force of the Mohawk, fought with the British. The American Revolution not only pitted the ancient foes of French and British soldiers against each other, but also ended hundreds if not thousands of years of peaceful coexistence and cooperation between the Iroquois.

WOMEN WERE ESSENTIAL TO THE SUCCESS OF THE AMERICAN REVOLUTION

W omen have been essential to the United States Armed Forces since before the United States Armed Forces even existed. The creation of the Continental Army in 1775 forbade women from enlistment as soldiers, but they served the forces in many ways. As cooks, tailors, and nurses, they kept the garrisons functioning. Despite the ban, some women disguised themselves as men in order to fight, while others risked their lives as spies and informants in the Culper Spy Ring, a network of civilians whose intelligence gathering became the most effective espionage operation of the war. Often overlooked, believed to be ignorant, or simply ignored by the men they served, these women worked as housekeepers, cooks, innkeepers and seamstresses to the British and risked their lives to convey messages to the Continental Army. Historians believe messages may have been conveyed using signals such as candles, flower arrangements, even drying laundry in specific order on clotheslines. The names of these courageous women are mostly lost to history, documented only as 'agents' in the surviving papers and missives of the Culper Spy Ring. However, some have since been revealed. Historians have broken codes to reveal the names of three women who couriered secret messages for the Spy Ring: Anna

Strong, Sarah Townsend, sister of the spy Robert Townsend (code-name Samuel Culper, Jr.), and Mary Underhill, sister of spy ring operative Abraham Woodhull. One woman, known only as Agent 355, is often credited with providing information that exposed Benedict Arnold as a traitor to the Americans and supplied information leading to the arrest of Major John André.

18

ENSLAVED PERSONS FOUGHT FOR FREEDOM

T he Revolutionary War brought the promise of liberty not just for the British colonists, but also for the thousands of Black Americans who had been living in bondage. Slavery fuelled the fledgling economy of the new nation, with forced labour the dominant means of production on vast farms and plantations. This war, with its battle cry for liberty and justice for all, offered an opportunity to break free from the shackles of enslavement. The British enlisted over 20,000 African-descended soldiers with the assurance of freedom and farmland. The eventual loss of the war meant that thousands of Black Loyalists who had fought against the Americans were relocated worldwide throughout the British territories, including north into modern day Canada and as far away as Sierra Leone.

INITIALLY, the Continental Army did not enlist people of colour. Southern states feared it would lead to widespread emancipation, which would cripple their economies and way of life. By the late 1770s, however, General George Washington and the Patriot forces faced dwindling enlistment and workforce. The decision to ban Black soldiers was overturned, with the promise of freedom granted at the end of one's military service. It's estimated that 5,000 to 8,000 African-descended soldiers fought on behalf of the Americans.

REGARDLESS OF WHICH side they fought for, these soldiers showed exceptional bravery and skill. Sadly, because of the lack of documentation, most of their crucial contributions were lost to our collective history. Today, modern historians are working to identify and commemorate these brave individuals. To learn more about the contributions of people of colour during the Revolutionary war, be sure to investigate the lives of other heroes whose names are being reclaimed and reintroduced to new generations. Among them are Black Loyalist soldier Colonel Tye, colonial hero Peter Salem, and the daring double agent James Armistead, whose devotion to the cause led his superior officer to write a compelling letter on behalf of Armistead to recognize him legally as a freeman. In thanks, the now freed Armistead changed his surname to that of his commanding officer, and became known as James Armistead Lafayette.

THE FIRST RHODE ISLAND REGIMENT BECOMES THE FIRST BLACK REGIMENT

When George Washington overturned the ban on Black soldiers in the Continental Army, the Rhode Island legislature was the first colonial government to legalize the enlistment of people of colour. Almost immediately, the First Rhode Island Regiment was formed. Consisting of 130 Black New Englanders and commanded by General John Sullivan, the regiment distinguished itself as a fighting force at the Battle of Newport and multiple skirmishes in Virginia. One French soldier at the time noted in his letters that of all the soldiers assembled in Virginia, it was the First Rhode Island Regiment that stood out repeatedly for their polished uniforms, comportment, and precision in maneuvers.

SALEM POOR DEFINED BRAVERY ON BUNKER HILL

Born into slavery in the 1740s, Salem Poor's resilience and courage led him to purchase his own freedom at age 20 for the notable sum of 27 pounds, a small fortune worth several thousand dollars today. With his hard-won freedom, Poor turned his efforts towards the liberty of others. He joined the Colonial army and fought at Saratoga, Monmouth, and, most famously, at the Battle of Bunker Hill. His bravery on the battlefield prompted no less than 14 fellow soldiers to formally petition The General Court of Massachusetts, requesting recognition of the man they called both brave and gallant in his efforts. They noted Poor's behaviour resembled that of an experienced officer, and credited him with the deaths of many enemy soldiers, including British Lieutenant Colonel James Abercrombie.

QUIZ TWO

The Players

TEST YOUR KNOWLEDGE

Now that you've learned 10 Fast Facts about many groups who fought during the American Revolution, here's a quick quiz to test your knowledge.

Question One:
Which of the following was NOT a nickname of the Continental Army:
a) Minutemen
b) Dutchmen
c) Washington's Army
d) Patriots

Question Two:
Which of the following was NOT a name for the British Forces:
a) Red Coats
b) The English
c) Royal Army
d) The Crown

Question Three:

What language did most Hessians speak:

a) French

b) Spanish

c) Russian

d) German

Question Four:

Which of the following was NOT a French soldier serving in the Continental Army:

a) General de Vimeur

b) Compte de Rochambeau

c) King Louis XVI

d) Admiral de Grasse

Question Five:

Which powerful alliance of six Native American nations was divided by the American Revolution:

a) Ojibwe

b) Iroquois

c) Chippewa

d) Mi'kmaw

Question Six:

Which of the following was NOT a French soldier serving in the Continental Army:

a) General de Vimeur

b) Compte de Rochambeau

c) King Louis XVI

d) Admiral de Grasse

Question Seven:

Which of the following were women NOT allowed to serve as by the Continental Army:

a) Nurses

b) Soldiers

c) Spies

d) Cooks

Question Eight:

Britain enlisted 20,000 African-descended soldiers during the American Revolution. Where did many of these men, called Black Loyalists, relocate to after the War:

a) France

b) Spain

c) Mexico

d) Canada

Question Nine:

Which colonial government was the first to legalize the enlistment of people of colour:

a) New York

b) Massachusetts

c) Maryland

d) Rhode Island

Question Ten:

Which battle did distinguished soldier Salem Poor not take part in:

a) Yorktown

b) Bunker Hill

c) Saratoga

d) Monmouth

Answers:

1. **Answer:** B, Dutchmen
2. **Answer:** C, Royal Army
3. **Answer:** D, German
4. **Answer:** C, King Louis XVI
5. **Answer:** B, Iroquois

6. Answer: C, King Louis XVI

7. Answer: B, Soldiers

8. Answer: D, Canada

9. Answer: D, Rhode Island

10. Answer: A, Yorktown

PARAGRAPH WRITING: THE PLAYERS

Using the facts we found on the previous pages, use the 8x8 model to write your own paragraph based on the prompts below. As you write the paragraph, remember to use the foolproof formula for paragraph writing. It goes like this:

Topic Sentence (TS)
    To begin with
    For Example
    Next
    Additionally
    This clearly shows
    Finally
    Closing Sentence (CS) with Concluding Phrase (CP)

There are many other transitional phrases that you can use instead of "To begin with", "Next", and "Finally". Try using some of the following in your paragraphs.
    Instead of "To begin with" try:

- First,

- Firstly,
- First of all,

Instead of "Next", try using:

- Second,
- Secondly,
- Another consideration,
- Furthermore,

Instead of "Finally", try using:

- Lastly,
- Thirdly,
- Most importantly,
- A final consideration

Question Prompts:

1. How were many Europeans involved in the American Revolution?
2. American colonists were not the only ones fighting the Revolutionary War. Discuss three other groups who fought against British Forces.
3. The Revolutionary War divided many groups of people. Describe how the war divided those living in the colonies.

PART III

American Revolution
Who's Who

WHO'S WHO OF THE AMERICAN REVOLUTION

Founding father Benjamin Franklin famously wrote to his friend the Scottish businessman and former Member of Parliament William Strahan about "an American planter, who had never seen Europe, was chosen by us to Command our Troops, and continued during the whole War. This man sent home to you, one after another, five of your best generals, baffled, their Heads bare of Laurels, disgraced even in the Opinion of their Employers."

What was the name of that planter? Which generals were defeated? And who were the distinguished men and women that changed the course of history as a result of their patriotism, courage, and dedication to the cause of democracy and freedom?

CRISPUS ATTUCKS WAS THE FIRST CASUALTY OF THE AMERICAN REVOLUTION

Thousands died as a result of the War of Independence, but Crispus Attucks was the first. On March 5, 1770, mounting tensions between colonial sailors and British servicemen erupted into violence known as the Boston Massacre. Of the five colonists killed in Boston harbour that day, witnesses named Crispus Attucks as the first victim, shot twice in the chest by British muskets. Attucks, a sailor and rope maker, was of African and First Nations descent and had escaped slavery in the Southern states. In Boston, he had supported the colonial sailors and resisted the British. With his death, Attucks became the first martyr for freedom during the Revolutionary War.

GEORGE WASHINGTON DIDN'T CHOP DOWN A CHERRY TREE - BUT HE DID RAISE AN ARMY

T he legend of a young George Washington being so virtuous he couldn't lie to his father about chopping down a tree is popular in descriptions of America's first president, but it isn't actually true. In fact, we know very little about his early life. He was born on February 22, 1732, to a wealthy landowner in British-controlled Virginia, where he learned basic subjects like history and math. When he was 11, his father died. His older half-brother Lawrence returned from England to help raise him, but there is little on record about that time. We know more about Washington's early adulthood, as he enlisted in the military in his 20s and served in the French and Indian War in the Ohio River Valley territory. Later colonists elected Washington, now a war hero, to the local government, called the colonial legislature. Here he spoke out against unfair laws and high taxes. It was 1775, five years after the Boston Massacre, when the colonies formed an army to fight against British rule and declare their independence. They chose Washington to lead it.

FOR FIVE TUMULTUOUS YEARS, the Revolutionary war raged on. Its impact stretched as far away as India and Africa. Despite many challenges, shortages of men and supplies, and harsh weather, Washington led the Continental Army to a decisive victory at Yorktown, Virginia. The British surrendered. Celebrated as a war hero and unanimously elected president of the newly formed United States of America, Washington set about creating the world's first modern republican government. After serving two terms, Washington stunned the world by stepping away from his power and retiring to his country home, Mount Vernon. Americans were then free to elect a new president. It would set the model for future presidential elections and term limits.

So WHERE DOES the story of the cherry tree come from? After Washington died in 1799, there was a tremendous demand for books about his life. Biographer Mason Locke Weems, who had never met Washington, invented the story of the young boy chopping down a tree and, when confronted by his angry father, told the truth instead of lying to avoid punishment. Weems knew Washington was a role model, especially for young Americans, so he invented the story as a lasting lesson in the virtue of honesty. It worked! The myth of the cherry tree continues in popular culture, movies, and books.

23

LAFAYETTE: THE AMERICAN WAR HERO WAS ACTUALLY A FRENCH ARISTOCRAT

S eventeen-year-old Gilbert du Motier attended a dinner party in 1777 that would change the course of history. He had become the Marquis de Lafayette as a young boy following his father's death during the Seven Years' War with Britain. Also at the dinner that evening was the Duke of Gloucester, the younger brother of England's King George III. The duke had fled to France after angering the king for marrying without permission. At dinner, the angry duke insulted his brother the king and praised the liberty-seeking American colonists who had fought the British at Lexington and Concord. Inspired and seeking his own revenge against the country that had killed his father, the young Marquis soon headed to America to fight for General Washington.

FORBIDDEN BY FRANCE TO FIGHT, little ability to speak English and no military experience, the Marquis was not much of a soldier at first. Yet, his courage and determination were clear. During his first conflict, the 1777 Battle of Brandywine, he was shot in the leg yet still coordinated a skillful retreat. As he recuperated, the Marquis studied military tactics. Once recovered, he took command of his own division. The rest, as they say, is history. Lafayette fought alongside Washington, endured the harsh winter at Valley Forge, and celebrated in the ultimate victory at Yorktown. Washington considered the Marquis a trusted commander and friend, and praised him for his dedication to the cause of liberty. Washington gave Lafayette honorary American citizenship, but the fighting Frenchman knew his battle for liberty hadn't ended.

LAFAYETTE RETURNED TO FRANCE. He fought in the French Revolution, and co-authored France's Declaration of the Rights of Man and Citizen, inspired by the American Declaration of Independence and Constitution. During the chaos known as the Reign of Terror, Austrian soldiers captured and imprisoned Lafayette as he fled for his life. France's new leader negotiated his release and paid his ransom, none other than Napoleon Bonaparte. Although grateful for his personal freedom, Lafayette refused to join Napoleon's government. He could not abandon his belief in liberty and equality. Lafayette spoke publicly against the elevation of Napoleon to emperor, arguing it was no better than the monarchy France had just overthrown. In the end, as Napoleon's ambitions spiraled out of control, it was Lafayette who convinced the people of France to reject the emperor and send him into exile, thus preserving the individual rights and freedoms Lafayette had spent his life fighting for.

24

PAUL REVERE WAS MORE THAN JUST A MIDNIGHT RIDER

P atriot Paul Revere is best known for his midnight ride to warn of a British invasion, but his contributions go well beyond that courageous night. In 1756, Revere had served in the provincial army during the French and Indian War, but by the mid 1760s, his loyalty to Britain had soured. Revere was a merchant and renowned silversmith, and the tariffs imposed by England hurt his business. So Revere joined the Sons of Liberty, and took part in protests against the Stamp Act, the first of many taxes that ignited the colonists' fervour to fight against taxation without representation. Revere was also part of an elaborate system of covert intelligence and early warning, the now famous 'one if by land, two if by sea' practice of hanging lanterns at the appointed time to indicate British troops were nearby. In 1773, he disguised himself as a First Nations warrior and took part in the Boston Tea Party. In 1775, Revere traveled to Concord to warn the patriots of nearby British troops and to help them move their military equipment. With his skill as an engraver, Revere helped to spread revolutionary ideas, creating etchings of popular propaganda paintings and reprinting them for wide distribution. The most famous of these comes from a drawing by Henry Pelham and depicts British soldiers taking close aim at the colonists.

Copies of Revere's prints still exist today. When war finally broke out, Revere enlisted in the Continental Army and put in command of the defence of Castle William in Boston Harbour. It was his industriousness, however, that best served the army. Revere constructed a much-needed powder mill to supply the soldiers and continued to craft weapons in his smithery.

DESPITE ALL THESE ACCOMPLISHMENTS, it was his brave ride through the night to warn of impending invasion, however, for which Revere will forever be remembered. On April 18th, 1775, as garrisons of soldiers boarded ships intent on raiding Concord, Revere sent word to Old North Church to hang the infamous warning lanterns, then set out on horseback with two other riders, Samuel Prescott and William Dawes, to warn the citizens and minutemen of the impending attack. Revere charged to Lexington, where he persuaded revolutionary leaders Samuel Adams and John Hancock to escape the city. They did. Revere was not so lucky. He was captured, questioned, and eventually released by the British, but not before they punished him with a beating and confiscated his horse.

DURING HIS LIFETIME Revere was many things - a renowned artisan, devout patriot, father of 16 children, a dentist, an engraver, entrepreneur and industrialist - but it was his 'Midnight Ride', memorialized in the poem by Henry Wadsworth Longfellow, for which he will go down in history.

25

SONS OF LIBERTY THREW MORE THAN JUST A TEA PARTY

Although details on the founding of this secretive group of colonists are unclear, the origin of the name begins not with an American, but an Irishman. Isaac Barré was a member of the British Parliament, but he was born and raised in Ireland. Like the Americans, the Irish lived under British rule and so it's not surprising that Barré was sympathetic to the concerns of the colonists and often spoke out on their behalf. During a 1765 debate over the Stamp Act, Barré referred to the colonists as "These Sons of Liberty" and the name stuck. The Sons organized protests and carried out extreme forms of civil disobedience. From threats and vandalism to all-out looting and violent riots, these provocateurs and radicals operated under the motto 'No Taxation Without Representation.'

THE STAMP ACT was in place for just a month when the Sons broke into the home of Andrew Oliver, the official stamp collector, and looted it. They demanded his public resignation - or else. Terrified, Oliver marched through the streets in a rainstorm to a spot known as the Liberty Tree in the town square. There he loudly quit his job before a cheering crowd of 2000 people. Next, the Sons coordinated their efforts in Boston and New York, with chapters quickly spreading to all 13 colonies. Frustrating the British at every opportunity, they destroyed the home of Thomas Hutchinson, the Lieutenant Governor and Chief Justice of Massachusetts, smashed windows of shop-keepers who sold British goods, and smeared filth and excrement on the homes of British Loyalists. When Britain imposed new tariffs on imported goods, Sons' leader Samuel Adams, a wealthy brewer and Harvard graduate, organized an official boycott of all British imports. Often those who didn't comply were beaten, kidnapped and held for days, or subjected to the terrible torture of hot tar and feathering.

WHILE THE PROTEST known as the Boston Tea Party went down in history as the most famous action of the Sons of Liberty, their ongoing secret network of rebels, disruptors, and all-out hooliganism undermined British rule and inspired the colonists to fight for freedom.

26

STAR SPANGLED SPY RING

While soldiers battled with bayonets and musket fire, there was a whole other war being waged with invisible ink, secret ciphers, and code names as the Culper Spy Ring secretly sent information from inside British strongholds to Washington and his allies. Formed by Benjamin Tallmadge, head of the Continental Army's secret service, the Culper Ring was first composed of Tallmadge's network of friends and relatives in Setauket, Long Island, when Britain took control of New York City in 1778. As they tracked British troop movements, the spies soon discovered British plans to ambush French troops arriving in Rhode Island and got word out to Washington in time to avoid the trap. From that early success, the spy ring slowly grew to include operatives throughout the colonies, composed of individuals who had access to British troops but weren't considered a threat, such as servants, innkeepers, and tailors. Notable among these was Hercules Mulligan, the Irish-American tailor who had taken in the orphaned Alexander Hamilton when he arrived in 1773 to attend King's College. Mulligan was married to the daughter of a Royal Navy officer, and British soldiers would openly talk with him about military matters as he repaired their uniforms at his successful tailoring shop. In Mulligan's homeland of Ireland, English rule had devastated the people and the land for over three hundred years. Although outwardly cooperative, Mulligan had no loyalty or love for the British. Together with his brother, Hugh, a contractor for the British Army, and Cato, a man whom Mulligan owned as an enslaved person, he collected information on the British and passed it on through the spy ring. The Culper Spy Ring was successful in preventing planned assassinations of Washington and other leaders. They uncovered tactical plans of the British Forces. Washington insisted upon intense secrecy within the spy ring. Not even he knew the identities of all of his informants. Today, the names of many of the operatives are still unknown, including that of Agent 355, the female spy who exposed Benedict Arnold as a defector.

27

THOMAS JEFFERSON FOUND OTHER
WAYS TO FIGHT

T homas Jefferson was many things - third President of the United States, author of the Declaration of Independence, architect, lawyer, farmer, secretary of state - but soldier was not one of them. During the Revolutionary War, Thomas Jefferson served in the Continental Congress, and from 1779 to 1781 he served as Governor of Virginia. A wealthy landowner, prominent politician, and prolific writer, Jefferson served the Continental Army through his numerous connections and publications, as well as considerable financial support. As a legislator, he rewrote laws in Virginia, drafting 126 bills in just three years, ending feudal property laws and introducing both religious freedom and public education. When the United States gained the Independence Jefferson wrote of in the 1776 Declaration of Independence, he served the new nation as its Secretary of State, then Vice President, and then became the third President of the United States. While he didn't arm himself on the battlefield, Jefferson waged a war of words for freedom that would shape not only America's liberty, but would become the rallying cry for national independence around the world.

. . .

DESPITE HIS MANY contributions to the creation of the United States, Jefferson is a complex and controversial figure in American history. Although he fought for personal liberties and civil rights, this did not extend to the enslaved population. Along with 5,000 acres of land known as Monticello, Jefferson also inherited 40 slaves on his 21st birthday. He later inherited another 135 slaves from his father-in-law. Over the course of his lifetime, Jefferson owned over 600 enslaved persons. He bought and sold many, and freed only seven. Modern students and historians recognize but cannot reconcile the disconnect between these two philosophies. It was a criticism Jefferson faced during his lifetime, too. Notably, founding fathers John Adams and Alexander Hamilton frequently criticized Jefferson for his participation in the enslavement of some while fighting for the liberty of others.

28

THE FIRST LADY FIRST FOUGHT FOR WOMEN'S RIGHTS

Seventeen-year-old Abigail Smith was not like the other girls her age. Born and raised in colonial Massachusetts, she could speak and read French, loved Shakespeare, and had an encyclopedic knowledge of history. So when her tutor introduced her to 28-year-old John Adams, an up-and-coming local lawyer with political aspirations, Abigail left quite an impression. The two soon exchanged long letters, a practice they would continue throughout their lives, and after the lengthy engagement her parents insisted upon, they wed.

As JOHN ADAMS rose in political rank, as an ambassador, vice president, and ultimately the 2nd President of the United States, Abigail was his closest confidant and greatest supporter. Raising their four children and overseeing the family farm on her own, Abigail Adams was also an early advocate for women's rights, the education of females, and the abolition of slavery. She argued passionately for the independence of the United States, as well as the hope such freedom should also apply to its female citizens. As the revolutionary war waged on, Abigail Adams bore witness to countless historic occasions, including the Battle of Bunker Hill, which she and her children watched from atop Penn's Hill nearby. Although her son, John Quincy, later recalled his mother sobbing at the loss of life, he said she felt it was her duty to witness the fight for freedom she so ardently supported. She was a trusted correspondent not only to her husband but also to several other prominent revolutionaries, including Martha Washington and Thomas Jefferson. The most famous of Adams' letters encouraged her husband and the other authors of the Constitution to 'Remember the ladies... and be more generous and favourable to them than your ancestors." She warned that women "will not hold ourselves bound by any Laws in which we have no Voice, or Representation." Critics of the outspoken Abigail took to calling her Mrs. President, although while her husband held office, she ceased all political correspondences in difference to his position.

A WOMAN of many historic titles including the first Second Lady of the United States, the second First Lady, and the first to live in the White House in Washington, DC, Abigail Adams was also the first woman to be both wife to, and then mother of, two different US presidents. Her son, John Quincy Adams, became the president in 1825.

29

KING GEORGE III COULDN'T ACCEPT DEFEAT

I f there is a villain in the story of the American Revolution, it is almost certainly King George III. One of the longest-serving British monarchs, King George ruled for 59 years and throughout his reign, he battled with the United States. However, it was the British parliament, and not the king, who created measures such as the Stamp Act and the Coercive Acts that set in motion the War of Independence. These laws, and the punishment for failure to obey them, infuriated the Americans and ultimately led to revolution. While restrictions on colonists were the work of parliament, they found a loud supporter in King George. He voiced his approval of the harsh measures in several declarations and condemned rebellious Americans he considered ungrateful traitors.

THE AMERICANS HURLED BACK their own insults. In his book *Common Sense*, Thomas Payne referred to the king as a 'royal brute', while the Declaration of Independence blamed the king directly in its twenty-seven grievances. The Declaration states that he had "plundered our seas, ravaged our Coasts, burnt our towns, and destroyed the lives of our people" as well as neglecting his duty to govern the people of the colonies justly and fairly.

IN THE END, Britain lost the war with the Americans, but defeat wasn't something the king could accept. He considered the 1777 loss at Saratoga a mere setback and didn't acknowledge the 1781 surrender at Yorktown as a definitive blow to British Forces. When his parliament drafted its peace terms for the Treaty of Paris, the king declared he would rather give up his throne than accept defeat. Although ultimately convinced to both accept the terms of the Treaty and continue as monarch, King George never truly accepted the loss. The two countries were at war again during the War of 1812, which ended in a stalemate. As he grew older, the king became increasingly unstable, delusional, and suffered from dementia. During the 'madness of King George,' he often engaged in loud, imaginary arguments with his long since retired prime minister, furious about his inability to control the American colonies.

30

CORNWALLIS LOST AMERICA BUT DEFEATED NAPOLEON

W hile the name Cornwallis is synonymous with defeat in the United States, Europeans regarded him as a capable general who governed both India and Ireland, and stood his ground against another very capable general, Napoleon Bonaparte. A British soldier and statesman, Cornwallis had openly opposed the British policies that so enraged the colonists. When duty called, however, he put aside his own opinions and took command of British forces during the American Revolution. Cornwallis successfully drove Washington and his Colonial Army out of New Jersey in 1776, and won a decisive victory in South Carolina over General Horatio Gates in 1780. But it was Yorktown in 1781 where Cornwallis and his troops fell under the combined ground forces of George Washington, the comte de Rochambeau, and the French fleet commanded by comte de Grasse, preventing Cornwallis and his men from fleeing in retreat. The British capitulated and surrendered. It was the end of the war for Cornwallis, but just the start of his political career.

· · ·

UPON HIS RETURN TO ENGLAND, Cornwallis was well rewarded for his service. Appointed Governor-General of India, he introduced a number of laws, known as the Cornwallis Code, that ensured civil servants were well paid and corruption severely punished. From 1798 to 1801, he governed as viceroy of Ireland. In 1802, when England was facing a new foe in France named Napoleon Bonaparte, Cornwallis was sent to Amiens to establish peace. As Britain's plenipotentiary, Cornwallis negotiated the Treaty of Amiens, bringing a halt to the Napoleonic Wars.

QUIZ THREE

American Revolution
Who's Who

TEST YOUR KNOWLEDGE

Now that you've learned 10 Fast Facts about key individuals during the American Revolution, here's a quick quiz to test your knowledge.

Question One:
During which event in 1770 was Crispus Attuks fatally shot by the British:
    a) Boston Tea Party
    b) Battle of Monmouth
    c) Battle of Lexington
    d) Boston Massacre

Question Two:
Where does the apocryphal story of George Washington and the cherry tree come from:
    a) Washington's boyhood diary
    b) Letters to his older brother, Lawrence
    c) A biographer invented the story
    d) A servant told the story to a newspaper

Question Three:

Who inspired a teenaged Lafayette to avenge his father's death by fighting against Britain in the American Revolution:

    a) His mother, Marie Louise Jolie de La Rivière

    b) His friend, Alexander Hamilton

    c) The French King, Louis the XV

    d) King George's brother, the Duke of Gloucester

Question Four:

Paul Revere was an artisan, devout patriot, father of 16 children, a dentist, an engraver, entrepreneur and industrialist - but what is he best known for:

    a) His midnight ride to warn of British invasion

    b) His bravery during the French Indian War

    c) His propaganda paintings

    d) His defense of Castle William

Question Five:

Who gave the Sons of Liberty their name:

    a) Thomas Payne, author of Common Sense

    b) Isaac Barré, member of the British Parliament

    c) Charles Cornwallis, British General

    d) Samuel Adams, wealthy colonial business owner

Question Six:

Who did the Culper Spy Ring reveal as a traitor to the Continental Army:

    a) Hercules Mulligan

    b) Anne Strong

    c) Benjamin Tallmadge

    d) Benedict Arnold

Question Seven:

Which of the following did Thomas Jefferson NOT do:

    a) Owned enslaved persons

b) Became Secretary of State

c) Fought in the Revolutionary War

d) Served as a lawyer

Question Eight:

Abigail Adams was the second First Lady of the United States. Which of the following was she NOT the *first* woman to do:

a) Become both a wife and a mother of an American president

b) Live in the White House

c) Encourage the president to allow women to vote

d) Enlist in the Continental Army

Question Nine:

How many grievances against King George III are listed in the Declaration of Independence:

a) One hundred

b) Twenty-Seven

c) Fifty-Nine

d) Two

Question Ten:

Although defeated in the United States, where did Britain appoint General Cornwallis as governor general as a reward for his service:

a) Ireland

b) Amiens

c) England

d) India

Answers

1. **Answer:** D, Boston Massacre

2. **Answer:** C, A biographer invented the story

3. **Answer:** D, King George's brother, Duke of Gloucester

4. **Answer:** A, His midnight ride to warn of British invasion

5. **Answer:** B, Isaac Barré, member of British Parliament

6. **Answer:** D, Benedict Arnold

7. **Answer:** C, Fought in the Revolutionary War

8. **Answer:** D, Enlist in the Continental Army

9. **Answer:** B, Twenty-Seven

10. **Answer:** C, India

PARAGRAPH WRITING: WHO'S WHO

Using the facts we found on the previous pages, use the 8x8 model to write your own paragraph based on the prompts below. As you write the paragraph, remember to use the foolproof formula for paragraph writing. It goes like this:

Topic Sentence (TS)
    To begin with
    For Example
    Next
    Additionally
    This clearly shows
    Finally
    Closing Sentence (CS) with Concluding Phrase (CP)

Some paragraphs require you to take a position or show multiple perspectives. When you are asked to state your opinion consider changing your transitional phrases at the start of each sentence.

    Instead of "To begin with" try using:

- Although there were many factors, the most important was...
- Among the many factors, the first to consider is...
- While there were many perspectives, it is important to first include....
- There were many ways that (prompt) was important, including...

Question Prompts:

1. Describe the contributions of three individuals who did not serve as soldiers in the Revolutionary War.
2. Name two secret organizations and explain how they contributed to the success of the War of Independence.
3. One individual can have a large impact. Choose one individual from this section and describe the impact they have on history.

PART IV

Protests, Politics, and Policy During the American Revolution

PROTESTS, POLITICS, AND POLICY DURING THE AMERICAN REVOLUTION

The Enlightenment of the 1700s brought about great political and social change as new ideas about freedom of speech, equality, freedom of press, and religious tolerance spread from Europe to the North American colonies. Although they were British subjects, American colonists did not have the same rights as Britains living in England. When the British government refused to grant equal political status to their colonial subjects, rebellion soon led to revolution.

POLITICAL PROTESTORS KNEW HOW TO PARTY

I f you sent an RSVP to the event thrown on at Griffin's Wharf on December 16, 1773, in Boston, Massachusetts, it might not have been the kind of party you were expecting. After nearly a decade of taxation without representation, colonists were furious at the introduction of yet another new tax, this one on the importation of tea. The British parliament understood the colonists' frustrations, but weren't about to give up the revenue they earned on the 1.2 million pounds of tea sold to the colonies every year. In response, the colonists smuggled in Dutch tea, with familiar names like businessman and brewer Samuel Adams among the most notable smuggled tea dealers. Britain fought back, tightening laws around tea smuggling, allowing the British East India company to import tea at a cheaper rate and duty-free, and passing the taxes and tariffs on to the colonists. On December 16, three ships - The Dartmouth, the Beaver, and the Eleanor - were all in the Boston Harbor, loaded with a cargo of tea. Meanwhile, thousands of colonists arrived at the wharf to prevent the tea from being unloaded, stored, sold, used, or, most importantly, taxed. The appointed British governor, Thomas Hutchinson, refused to negotiate with the protestors and demanded payment of the tariffs and the tea unloaded. Neither side relented. It looked like there was going to be a weeks-long standoff between the governor and the colonists.

ENTER THE SONS OF LIBERTY. Although no one can definitely prove Samuel Adams's secretive band of disruptors were officially involved, among the hundreds still gathered at the wharf were a large, well-organized group of men dressed in what one participant, George Hewes, described as "in the costume of an Indian, equipped with a small hatchet." The men boarded the three ships and set about cutting open 340 chests of tea, weighing over 92,000 pounds or 46 tons, and tossing them into the water below. It took nearly three hours, and although £9,659 worth of tea - that's nearly 1.9 million dollars in today's money - was destroyed, British troops did not intervene and no one was injured. In fact, the rebels took great care not to harm anyone on board the ships and even swept up the loose tea leaves from the decks before they departed. The only reported damage was a broken padlock on a chest that belonged to a ship's captain. The next day, the captain received a new lock as repayment for his broken property.

WHOEVER THE PROTESTORS WERE, it was clear they were well organized and under strict orders to keep their composure, not resort to violence, and only to destroy the tea and nothing else. Afterwards, only one participant, Francis Akeley, was arrested and imprisoned. Much later George Hewes confessed his participation, but both refused to name their fellow rebels. Destruction of property was a serious crime, and many leading colonists felt the rebels had gone too far. George Washington wrote in his letters that the protestors "were mad" as in mentally unwell, while Benjamin Franklin personally offered to cover the cost of the destroyed merchandise. Both leaders felt the protestors had gone too far, and King George III agreed. As a result of the Boston Tea Party, the British parliament issued a series of harsh new laws and regulations known first as the Coercive Acts and, later, the Intolerable Acts in 1774.

32

PARLIAMENT PASSED THE INTOLERABLE ACTS

I f there was one thing the colonists couldn't tolerate, it was the Intolerable Acts. Passed by an angry British Parliament in retaliation for ongoing defiance by the American colonies, these new laws punished the colonists and reduced their political freedoms, if not stripped them away entirely. First, the Boston Port Bill of 1773 closed that city's lucrative harbour until restitution was made for the damage caused by the protest known as the Boston Tea Party. The 1774 Massachusetts Government Act went even further, reducing Massachusetts down to a crown colony, replacing its elected council with British appointees, abrogating the colonial charter, forbidding public meetings, and granting more power to the British military governor. Meanwhile, the aptly named Murder Act, aka the 1774 Administration of Justice Act, limited the legal rights guaranteed in the Magna Carta by allowing Crown officials who were accused of committing a crime, including murder, while carrying out "the execution of the law, or for the suppression of riots and tumults" to have their trials moved to England or another British colony that would be more likely to acquit them of their crimes. While it was parliament, not King George III, who passed these laws, they did so with the king's public support and his legal approval, called Royal Assent. To his colonial subjects, King George was no longer seen as merely a political figurehead, but as a tyrant stripping them of their legal rights.

33

NOT ALL COLONISTS WANTED
POLITICAL INDEPENDENCE

As violent conflict was breaking out in 1776, much of the population in the Thirteen Colonies were opposed to all-out war. Many colonists saw a corrupt parliament as their enemy, but were initially loyal to the young King. They hoped to have their own representatives installed in parliament who would in turn protect their interests. Plus, being British subjects had its benefits. With the British Army and Navy guarding its borders the colonies were protected from French or Spanish invasion. In Britain the colonies had a wealthy trade partner eager to buy their goods and protect their merchant ships, albeit with the high taxes and tariffs attached. During the early protests, conflict often erupted between the colonists themselves. The Sons of Liberty, for example, would target local businesses and individuals known for having strong ties and staunch support for Britain. Those colonists who opposed rebellion and, later, revolution and who wanted to continue on as British subjects were known as Loyalists. Other names included 'Royalists', 'Tories', or 'King's Men' in reference to King George III. Those who refused to declare for one side or the other were known as 'fence sitters'. Although not in favour of the war, following the surrender at

Yorktown and the withdrawal of British troops, 80 to 90% of Loyalists and fence sitters chose to remain in the United States once it became an independent nation.

34

ALL MEN ARE CREATED EQUAL. BUT THAT DIDN'T MEAN EVERYBODY

On July 4, 1776, the Continental Congress unanimously signed the Declaration of Independence, enacting their political autonomy with the words of Thomas Jefferson, *"...that all men are created equal, that they are endowed by their Creator with certain unalienable Rights, that among these are Life, Liberty and the pursuit of Happiness."* The Declaration is arguably one of the most important political documents ever written in the English language. While many modern students are familiar with these opening lines, few are able to recall the contents of the other 32 paragraphs of this historic text. In particular, students are often unfamiliar with the second last sentence, which states *"as Free and Independent States, they have full Power to levy War, conclude Peace, contract Alliances, establish Commerce, and to do all other Acts and Things which Independent States may of right do."* It's between these opening lines and closing sentences where the gap exists between who was, and who wasn't, considered equal under the law.

THE *"OTHER ACTS and Things which Independent States may of right do"* included determining who was and wasn't eligible to citizenship, legal protections, and who had the right to vote – which is called enfranchisement. The other "Free and Independent States" mentioned, such as France and the Netherlands, could legalize slavery or ban it, recognize females as whole persons or merely possessions, and provide protections for children or permit them to work hard labour. In other words, each country was free to make its own laws and the United States was prepared to fight for this same freedom. When independence as a nation was achieved and another historic document, The Constitution, was drafted, the United States government set to work enacting its own laws. Importantly, it also created mechanisms to add or to change these laws, also known as amendments. Subsequently, while slavery was legal and women were denied the right to vote when the Constitution came to force in 1789, the 13th, 14th, and 15th Amendments, enacted in the 1880s and known as the Civil War Amendments, prohibited slavery and granted voting rights to men regardless of their race, colour, or previous servitude and the 19th Amendment, enacted in 1920, granted American women the right to vote.

35

THE REVOLUTIONARY WAR DID NOT END SLAVERY

Although the Declaration of Independence announced to the world in 1776 that 'All men are created equal' it would be more than one hundred years later that slavery, the practice of legally enslaving another person into forced and unpaid labour, would end in the United States. During the Revolutionary War, African American slaves and former slaves fought on both sides. From the outset, Britain offered freedom to those who escaped slavery to serve with British forces. As tensions mounted in 1775, the last Royal Governor of Virginia, Lord Dunmore, offered freedom to those willing to turn on their captors and help put down the growing rebellion. As the chaos of war and the presence of British troops grew, so did opportunities for escape. During the conflict, 30% of the enslaved population of South Carolina migrated, escaped, or died in the fighting. Wealthy plantation owners in Southern states saw the loss of slaves, whom they considered property, not people, to be another attack on their economy by Britain, further fueling their fight for Independence. Modern historians point out the disconnect between those fighting for liberty while simultaneously enslaving others, but this isn't simply a modern perspective. Founding Fathers such as Alexander Hamilton, Benjamin Franklin, and John Jay served in antislavery societies and publicly criticized the practice. And while slavery was legal in every Northern colony at the beginning of the war, by the end the newly formed northern states rapidly began to forbid the practice.

THE IRONY of the American War of Independence is that for enslaved persons in the colonies, by and large it was the British who represented freedom, not their fellow colonists. The practice of legalized slavery had existed throughout history, and while it violated new ideals of personal liberties, it also fueled the colonies' newly emerging economies. It functioned and was legal, if unethical, and protected under the private property rights of those who still considered enslaved persons as property.

36

WAR BROUGHT UNWANTED HOUSE GUESTS

S
o much has been written about the battles of the American Revolution, but it's important to remember that during the war years most of the American population was not involved in the fighting. In fact, unless a battle was being waged nearby, normal life in American villages and towns continued on just as it had been before the Declaration of Independence. Merchants continued to buy and sell goods, tradesmen continued to craft their merchandise and sell their services, and farmers did the best they could to maintain their crops and livestock. While citizens tried to carry on with everyday life, it was hardly business as usual. Many found themselves the unfortunate victims of theft, abuse, or worse when an advancing army marched through. Even though both the British and American militaries had stringent rules and strict warnings against harming civilians, there were reports of soldiers on both sides taking grain, goods, or whatever they needed from nearby farms and plundering homes any valuables they could carry. Many records show the American officers ordered the confiscation of goods during particularly desperate times when their resources grew dangerously low, but promised homesteaders that they would repay what they took and kept an inventory of confiscated goods. The British, mean-

while, promised restitution but didn't specify how they would pay for what they took. Even Benjamin Franklin found himself the host of unwanted house guests. During the winter of 1777 a British officer seized Franklin's home in Philadelphia and made it his seasonal headquarters, helping himself not only to the warmth and comfort of the house, but taking many of Franklin's personal objects as souvenirs and spoils of war.

37

WASHINGTON SHOT HIS ENTIRE ARMY
— WITH A VACCINE

T he Revolution brought about numerous changes to American politics, including the end of nobility and feudalism and the introduction of enfranchisement to some new social groups. It also brought about changes in health care. Prior to the War of Independence it was disease, not combat, that brought about the death not only of soldiers but of entire encampments including nurses, cooks, doctors and other non-combat personnel. During the attempted invasion of Canada in 1775, smallpox ravaged American troops to the point John Adams wrote of the devastation "smallpox is ten times more terrible than the British, Canadian, and Indians together." George Washington himself had survived a terrifying bout of smallpox during his trip to Barbados when he was 19, and was lucky to survive. He knew that the American soldiers were more likely to die of smallpox than the British. The disease had existed in Europe for decades and many British soldiers had already contracted and survived it, but few Americans had been exposed to the disease. Only 23% of enlisted men from North Carolina, for example, had survived smallpox. Washington knew an outbreak would be devastating to his troops and to the outcome of the war. So, during the winter of 1777, when Washington had the means to inoculate the entire Continental Army, he made the bold and highly controversial decision to ensure the entire encampment received inoculation. It was a huge risk. After their inoculation shot, soldiers were often incapacitated for stretches of time, reducing the number of the functional army. Washington took great care to ensure the inoculation process was done in secrecy so as not to tip off the reduced numbers to the British forces. The plan worked. By the end of the year, smallpox deaths in the Continental Army had dropped from 17% to just 1%. As historian Elizabeth Hern put it "Washington's unheralded and little-recognized resolution to inoculate the Continental forces must surely rank with the most important decisions of the war." Washington's insistence on vaccination against smallpox legitimized the medical procedure and encouraged American citizens to do the same.

38

WASHINGTON WINTERS WITH HIS TROOPS AT VALLEY FORGE

On December 19th, 1777, George Washington led his troops into their winter camp. Located on a high plateau with strategic access to ample firewood and clean water, the advantageous spot would come to be known as one of the lowest periods for Continental Army - the Winter at Valley Forge. Comprised of 12,000 Continental soldiers, smaller numbers of African American and First Nations troops, and nearly 500 women and children, the army arrived tired, hungry and in low spirits, having suffered recent defeats at Brandywine, Paoli, and German-town despite their definitive victory of Saratoga just a few months before in September 1777. Washington swiftly surveyed both the barren campsite and his weary troops, nearly 3,000 of whom were shoeless, and ordered work to begin immediately before the freezing temperatures of January set in. The men built 12x12 wooden lodges, and filled them with hay for warmth and insulation. As supplies ran dangerously low, Washington sent a team led by Nathanael Greene to seek food and supplies from nearby farmsteads. Despite the terrible weather and lack of supplies, the Continental Army held together. Washington wrote in his letters that it was because his army was of "one heart" and "one mind", but contemporaries of the time cited

Washington's policy to stay among his troops and endure the same challenges that they did that inspired his army to withstand the winter. When Washington's wife, Martha, arrived in February 1888 to support her husband in the camp, it reinforced his men's belief that Washington would "share in the hardship" and "partake of every inconvenience," his army faced, and inspired them to carry on. The local population had originally feared the camp would bring debauchery and plunder, but under Washington's tight command the camp maintained its order and, as a result, enjoyed the generosity of neighboring farms.

ALTHOUGH VALLEY FORGE is best remembered for its hardships, the months in camp offered the continental army time to strategize and train. A young French officer, better known as the nobleman Marquis de Lafayette, arrived in camp and quickly set about organizing the Corps d'Etrangers, composed of officers from Poland, France, and other European nations. Meanwhile, the skilled Baron Friedrich von Steuben, who had distinguished himself in the Prussian army, took on the role of drillmaster, teaching Continental soldiers how to effectively use bayonets as well as combat strategy. By the spring the army was better trained, fed, and bolstered by news of France's support through the Franco-American alliance. On June 19th, 1778, six months after they had arrived, the Continental Army left Valley Forge headed to face the British at Monmouth.

39

THE AMERICAN REVOLUTION CREATED CANADA...SORT OF

T he Treaty of Paris of 1763 ended the European conflict known as the Seven Years' War and its corresponding North American conflict often referred to as the French Indian War. As a result new political borders were drawn up as France ceded its colonies, including the Canadian territories, known as New France and Quebec, the Great Lakes Basin, and the east bank of the Mississippi River to Britain. Along with the 13 American Colonies, there were also the colonies of Nova Scotia, New Brunswick, Prince Edward Island, and Newfoundland, and these new territories expanded British rule across much of the North American continent. Also in 1763, as unwieldy colonists pushed to expand their holdings westward, King George III issued a Royal Proclamation which, among other things, limited American expansion, defined the North American interior west of the Appalachian Mountains as a vast Indigenous reserve, and set out the legal structure for the negotiation of treaties with the Indigenous populations. By 1774, General Gage had taken military control over all of North America, but with him stationed in Boston and British troops widely dispersed, American forces began to attack the Canadian colonies in hopes of securing land and convincing the inhabitants to switch allegiances.

They were met with the staunch neutrality of the predominantly French speaking settlers who trusted neither the British nor the Americans and fierce opposition from the Indigenous populations. Then, in 1775, a disastrous attack during a snowstorm on December 31st resulted in 400 Americans captured, Benedict Arnold wounded, and the death of General Montgomery. The Americans retreated. Meanwhile, the colony of Nova Scotia was enjoying its elevated status and steady income as the North American port of operations for both the Royal Navy and the British Vice-Admiralty Court, ensuring the loyalty of its colonists to the British Crown throughout the War of Independence. With the exception of the failed invasion of Quebec in 1775–1776, the Revolutionary War had little effect on the Canadian colonies until the second Treaty of Paris, this one signed in 1783, ended the War. Soon, more than forty thousand Loyalists fled America, including numerous freed persons, those escaping slavery, and former indentured servants granted land and citizenship as payment for their service during the War, arrived in the Canadian colonies seeking a new life in a new land.

40

THE 4TH OF JULY WASN'T ALWAYS A HOLIDAY

I n fact, President John Adams believed Americans were celebrating the wrong date. He claimed that because the Continental Congress had voted on July 2nd, not the 4th, that was the real date of independence. Nonetheless, most Americans held their celebrations two days later, on July 4th, to celebrate the formal adoption of the Declaration of Independence. Early festivities included games, sports, and the ringing of church bells. In 1778, George Washington honoured the date by ordering double rations of rum for all his soldiers, and in 1781, months before the decisive Battle of Yorktown, the state of Massachusetts formally declared July 4th a state holiday. While in office, Thomas Jefferson hosted the first July 4th celebration at the White House in 1801. The rest of the country wasn't so quick. In fact, it took another 100 years and a Civil War before the U.S. Congress officially declared July 4th an unpaid federal holiday in 1871 and another 70 years and two World Wars before Congress expanded the provision to ensure employees were paid on the holiday. As for John Adams, he stuck to his beliefs and stubbornly refused any Independence Day celebrations held on July 4th, opting instead to host his own party on July 2nd.

QUIZ FOUR

Protests, Politics, and Policy During the American Revolution

TEST YOUR KNOWLEDGE

Now that you've learned 10 Fast Facts about the protests, politics, and policies of the American Revolution, here's a quick quiz to test your knowledge.

Question One:

Which of the following was NOT one of the three ships boarded during the Boston Tea Party:

a) The Eleanor

b) The Dartmouth

c) The Enterprise

d) The Beaver

Question Two:

What was the lethal sounding nickname of the 1774 Administration of Justice Act:

a) The Death Tax

b) The Murder Act

c) The Fatal Laws

d) The Joy Killer

Question Three:

Which of the following was NOT a nickname for colonists who did not want independence from Britain:

a) Royalists

b) King's Men

c) Loyalists

d) White Feathers

Question Four:

The mechanisms which enable American lawmakers to alter the Constitution are called:

a) Addendums

b) Abrogates

c) Amendments

d) Additions

Question Five:

During the American Revolution, what percentage of the enslaved population of South Carolina migrated, escaped, or died in the fighting:

a) 10%

b) 50%

c) 70%

d) 30%

Question Six:

During the winter of 1777 a British officer seized a Philadelphia home and made it his seasonal headquarters. Which Founding Father did it belong to:

a) George Washington

b) Thomas Jefferson

c) John Adams

d) Benjamin Franklin

Question Seven:

In 1775, John Adams wrote that this dangerous threat to the Continental Army was *"ten times more terrible than the British, Canadian, and Indians together."*

a) Spanish Pirates

b) The Royal Navy

c) Smallpox

d) Winter Snowstorms

Question Eight:

Who arrived at Valley Forge during the harsh winter and took on the role of training and commanding the Polish, French, and European soldiers:

a) Nathanael Green

b) Marquis de Lafayette

c) Alexander Hamilton

d) General Cornwallis

Question Nine:

Why did the Royal Proclamation of 1763 anger the American colonists:

a) It declared war on the American colonies

b) It established French as the official language of Canada

c) It granted Spain more territory in the east

d) It limited expansion west of the Appalachian Mountains

Question Ten:

President John Adams believed Americans were celebrating the wrong date as Independence Day. What date did Adams celebrate on:

a) July 1st

b) July 15th

c) July 2nd

d) July 31st

Answers

1. **Answer:** C, The Enterprise

2. **Answer:** B, The Murder Act

3. **Answer:** D, White Feathers

4. **Answer:** C, Amendments

5. **Answer:** D, 30% of the enslaved population of South Carolina migrated, escaped, or died in the fighting.

6. **Answer:** D, Benjamin Franklin

7. **Answer:** C, Smallpox

8. **Answer:** B, Marquis de Lafayette

9. **Answer:** D, Limited expansion west of the Appalachian Mountains

10. **Answer:** C, July 2nd.

PARAGRAPH WRITING: PROTESTS, POLITICS, AND POLICY DURING THE AMERICAN REVOLUTION

Using the facts we found on the previous pages, use the 8x8 model to write your own paragraph based on the prompts below. As you write the paragraph, remember to use the foolproof formula for paragraph writing. It goes like this:

Topic Sentence (TS)
    To begin with
    For Example
    Next
    Additionally
    This clearly shows
    Finally
    Closing Sentence (CS) with a Concluding Phrase (CP)

Some paragraphs will ask you to show cause and consequence. In other words, how one event led to another, or the impact an event had on people, places, and the environment. When asked to show cause and consequence, you can vary the 8x8 transition words at the start of your sentences. Try using the following:

- As a result of
- Due to the
- One outcome of (cause) was (the consequence)
- There were several consequences resulting from (cause), including
- One result of the (cause) was (consequence)

Question Prompts:

1. Who did the 1776 Declaration of Independence leave out in its demands for political and personal freedoms, and how did it exclude them?
2. How did the political actions of Britain result in the American Revolution?
3. What policies and political actions did the Thirteen Colonies take to establish themselves as independent from British Rule?

PART V

Battles
&
The Military

BATTLES & THE MILITARY

Britain thought the conflict would be quashed within a matter of months. After all, the inexperienced and amateur colonial Minutemen versus the greatest military force on the planet looked like a fight between a mouse and lion. Yet from the moment the 'shot heard round the world' rang out, it was clear that the conflict between American colonists and the British forces would be a fight for freedom wherein patriotic men and women were willing to risk everything, including their lives.

41

THE BOSTON MASSACRE - 1770

Tensions were running high in Boston in 1770, as 2,000 British soldiers occupied the city and tried to enforce Britain's unpopular tax laws on its population of 16,000 colonists. Protests were common as the angry colonists, called patriots, took out their frustration by vandalizing stores selling British goods and intimidating their neighbours with loyalist leanings. On a snowy night in March 1770, British private Hugh White stood as the lone guard outside the Custom House on King Street. He was soon joined by a small gang of angry protestors, who first hurled insults at him before moving on to snowballs and eventually rocks. At that point, White rang the bell for help. It arrived in the form of his commander, Captain Thomas Preston, and several soldiers. Rather than quieting the situation, tensions grew, as the protestors began to punch the soldiers and hit them with clubs. At some point, someone said 'fire' - it is unclear if it was an order from Preston or a plea from someone in the mob. A bullet cut through the crowd, felling Crispus Attauks, an escaped slave who had been working at the Boston dockyards. Soon several more shots were fired, killing four more men.

· · ·

PRESTON and his men were arrested and tried for murder. Their defense lawyer was none other than future President of the United States John Adams, who was able to secure a 'not guilty' verdict for Preston and a lesser conviction of manslaughter for the accused soldiers. Fuelled by the writings and propaganda of the Sons of Liberty, the event came to be known as the Boston Massacre, and Crispus Attucks the first victim of the Revolutionary War.

THE SHOT HEARD ROUND THE WORLD - 1775

Although it had rained early in the day, by the evening of April 18th, 1775, the air was dry and cool and ideal for riding. Two expeditions set off from Boston that night that would change the course of history. The first was a battalion of British soldiers, hundreds of troops marching toward Concord, Massachusetts where American colonists had stockpiled weapons and ammunition. The British were on order to seize the armory and take the supplies for themselves. The second journey consisted of a lone man on his horse, intent on making it to Concord before the British to warn his fellow colonists. His name was Paul Revere. As morning broke on April 19th, 1775, the British reached the town of Lexington, where a militia of approximately 70 men, warned by Paul Revere, were armed and gathered on the village green. To this day, no one knows for certain who fired the first shot, but by the end of the fighting eight Americans were dead, an equal number were wounded, and one British soldier was shot. Later the poet Ralph Waldo Emerson would memorialize the moment in poetry as 'The Shot Heard Round the World'.

THE BATTLES OF LEXINGTON &
CONCORD 1775

F ollowing the fighting at Lexington, the British troops continued on to Concord, intent on capturing the Americans' cache of weapons and subduing any rebels along the way. Warned by Paul Revere, who had ridden through the night to warn the town, an angry resident militia stood at the ready. The 700 British troops broke apart into companies to search the town for the supplies. At 11:00am at the town's North Bridge, a company of 100 British Regulars were met by 400 armed militiamen. Gunfire erupted, with casualties taken on both sides. Outnumbered, the soldiers fell back from the bridge and rejoined the now retreating British forces. As the British began their march back to Boston, they were harassed by heavy fire from the militia of neighbouring towns, taking casualties until they were safely back within the city. But the minutemen weren't done. Once the British troops were back in the city, the accumulated militias formed a blockade across the narrow land access to the cities of Charlestown and Boston, beginning the nearly year-long siege of Boston. The American Revolutionary War had truly begun.

44

THE CONTINENTAL ARMY IS FORMED - 1775

By June 14, 1775, it was clear to Congress that the only remaining solution for the American Colonies was to meet the British in the theatre of war. But who would lead this inexperienced, ill-supplied group of militiamen into battle against the largest, most capable military force in the world? One stood above the rest, literally. At over six feet, and attending the proceedings in his military uniform, George Washington not only looked the part, but was one of the few candidates who had the leadership skills and experience commanding troops from his time serving in the French and Indian War. His experience was limited, however. He had never had more than 2000 under his command and the demands of maneuvering large formations of infantry, strategic use of cavalry or artillery, or procuring the thousands of supplies needed for men in the field were new to him. Nonetheless, Washington proved to be the man for the job. Helming the army for eight years, Washington oversaw a fighting force that averaged 48,000 men at any given time. Turnover and desertion were constant problems, particularly during the harsh winter months, and the soldiers were paid not in money but in grants and promissory notes. In a show of solidarity with his troops, Washington refused to take a salary, asking only that

Congress cover his expenses. From a distance, it must have appeared absurd, like a mouse fighting a lion. But, in the end, under Washington's skillful leadership the Continental Army emerged victorious and, as Benjamin Franklin famously wrote, *"an American planter, who had never seen Europe, was chosen by us to Command our Troops, and continued during the whole War. This man sent home to you, one after another, five of your best generals, baffled, their Heads bare of Laurels, disgraced even in the Opinion of their Employers."*

45

THE CONTINENTAL NAVY IS FORMED - 1775

W hile most students are familiar with land battles like Bunker Hill and Yorktown, the Revolutionary War was also fought on water - both the Atlantic Ocean to the East and the Great Lakes to the North. By October 1775, George Washington had already taken measures to secure ships to transport his men and supplies, and he found an ally in John Adams who argued strenuously in Congress for the creation of a naval force. Congress agreed, directing Adams to draft out the regulations and authorizing the construction of thirteen frigates within the next three months, including five ships with 32 guns, five more armed with 28 guns, and three 24-gun boats in December 1775. As the small fleet could never outrun or outgun the British, the Continental Navy first focused its attention on interrupting the supply to Britain, while helping themselves to the goods. The first major success came swiftly, in March 1776, in a brief battle on the water near Nassau, Bahamas, where the Continentals secured valuable shipments of gunpowder. In the North, Benedict Arnold commissioned 12 war vessels to combat British invasion from the Canadian colonies. Although all 12 ships were lost, the Continental Navy sufficiently delayed Britain from sending reinforcements and supplies. The Navy wasn't completely outmatched, however, as France loaned sailors and vessels to the Continentals until, in 1778, it officially joined the War and sent in its fleet. John Paul Jones, perhaps the best-known captain of the Continental Navy, left his mark on history when his frigate, Bonhomme Richard, came up against the man-of-war HMS Serapis. During the fighting, Jones lost several guns and the rigging of the two ships became entangled, damaging the Richard. When Serapis' captain asked if Jones was ready to surrender, the American replied *"I have not yet begun to fight!"* With that, Jones and his crew boarded the Serapis, fought the men into submission, and captured the ship.

46

THE BATTLE OF BUNKER HILL WASN'T ACTUALLY FOUGHT ON BUNKER HILL - 1775

The battle we all know as Bunker Hill wasn't, in fact, fought on Bunker Hill. It actually took place about one-third of a mile south of Bunker Hill, Massachusetts, on Breeder's Hill. On that hot June 17 in 1775, the newly formed American Continental Army suffered its first defeat just days after it had officially been formed. As Major-General William Howe and 2200 British troops marched in well trained columns towards the battleground, the outgunned and outnumbered Colonel William Prescott ordered his 1000 men to hold their fire 'until you see the whites of their eyes.' With just a few yards between them, the Americans fired a lethal barrage from their muskets, breaking the Redcoat lines. After a brief retreat, the British reformed and attacked, and were once again met by patriot musket fire. By their third assault, the patriots were low on ammunition, though, and as the British climbed the hill they were met with hand-to-hand combat from the Americans until Prescott ordered the retreat. It was one of the bloodiest engagements of the war. The Patriots had killed more than 200 soldiers, with another 800 injured by gunfire. Over 100 Americans perished, and another 300 lay wounded. Although the inexperienced army had lost the battle, their courage and their confidence let the British know victory would not be easily won. A few weeks later, on July 2, 1775, George Washington arrived to take command of the Continental Army.

THE BATTLES OF SARATOGA - 1777

For many historians, the Battles of Saratoga were the turning point of the Revolutionary War. Fought just eighteen days apart, the two battles had very different outcomes. On September 19th, 1777, the First Battle of Saratoga was fought on Freeman's Farm with the British taking the definitive victory after a day of fierce fighting. Although a win, it came at a cost, as several British soldiers were injured while the hired German troops were called in to support the faltering British line. The British commander, John Burgoyne, made the decision to stay put and wait for reinforcements as his men recovered. It was a tactical error. The Continental Army, commanded by General Horatio Gates, also decided to camp close by and were soon met with additional troops, bringing their numbers to 13,000. On October 7th, with supplies running low and no sign of help on the way, Bourgoyne decided to move his men north where the weakened army met the American forces at Bemis Heights. Heavy rain and freezing temperatures slowed the British, and soon they were surrounded and forced to surrender. Not only was the victory a needed boost for Continental Army, but their success helped to convince the French government to end its public neutrality and openly supply the Americans with military assistance.

THE BATTLES OF TRENTON & PRINCETON - 1776-1777

Everyone knows Washington crossed the Delaware during the freezing night of December 26, 1776, thanks in large part to the iconic painting by Emanuel Leutze. What isn't as commonly known is that Washington stealthily crossed the Delaware not once but *twice* to gain a surprise victory. Washington led his army across the icy waters of the Delaware River on Christmas night, leading his troops against the British-commanded German troops stationed at Trenton. Washington and his 1400 soldiers captured more than 900 men in a sneak attack and surprise victory. Then, having lured the British forces south, Washington led another daring night raid on January 3rd, 1777, to capture Princeton. Washington's cunning and courage, along with the decisive wins for his army, boosted the morale of the troops and reinforced their faith in the fight for their freedom.

THE BATTLE OF MONMOUTH - 1778

By June 28th, 1778, George Washington had held command of the Continental Army for just over three years. In that time he and his men had faced enemy forces, smallpox, harsh winters and dwindling supplies, but one of the most difficult challenges to overcome was infighting among his troops. General Charles Lee, Washington's second in command, was just such a challenge. That June, Washington had ordered Lee, who was second in command, to lead a small force out in front of the Continental Army to engage, distract, and annoy the Redcoats until the Continental forces could be assembled from Valley Forge. Lee disagreed with the plan but followed orders; however, after several hours of fighting he pulled his men back. Just as Lee was retreating with his men on the road near Monmouth Courthouse, New Jersey, he came across none other than his commander, Washington. Not known as a man who frequently or publicly lost his temper, it was clear that Washington was furious that Lee had disobeyed him. After angry words were exchanged, Lee once again led the advance party while Washington himself marched his troops. Under Washington's command, the patriots attacked the retreating British, earning another victory and praise for the courage and cool-headed leadership of Washington.

THE BATTLE OF YORKTOWN - 1781

The Battle of Yorktown, also known as The Siege of Yorktown, was the last major battle of the American Revolutionary War and, fittingly, is the last fact in this book! It began on September 28th, 1781, and ended thirty-two days later when the Continental Army, led by General George Washington and backed by both French troops and the French Navy, captured General Charles Cornwallis and the British forces in Yorktown, Virginia. Cornwallis, who held the rank of general and was also a British lord, was a respected military commander with a contingent of 9000 British troops when he found himself surrounded by the Washington-led ground force of 17,000. To the east in the harbour, the French naval forces prevented an escape by sea. For three weeks, both day and night, each side bombarded the other until, as supplies ran low, the British were forced to admit defeat and begin negotiations for surrender and retreat. At a formal surrender ceremony, Cornwallis handed over his sword to the French and American commanders on October 19, 1781. One popular story which emerged from that day, although historians can't prove it as a fact, is that the British military band played the song 'The World Turned Upside Down' as they marched away in surrender, and indeed it had. The world's mightiest military force had been defeated by an inexperienced patchwork of militiamen, farmers, and merchants, and the Old World order of monarchy gave way to a new form of a democratic republic.

QUIZ FIVE

Battles
&
The Military

TEST YOUR KNOWLEDGE

Question One

The soldiers who fired into the crowd during the Boston Massacre were defended by which lawyer:

a) Alexander Hamilton

b) Aaron Burr

c) John Adams

d) Thomas Jefferson

Question Two

How many American colonists were killed in Lexington in 1775, during the infamous 'Shot Heard Round the World'?

a) 3

b) 10

c) 1

d) 8

Question Three

At Concord, where did 100 British Regulars battle with 400 Minutemen?

a) The South Tower

b) The East Gate

c) The West Road

d) The North Bridge

Question Four

On average, how many soldiers were there in the Continental Army under George Washington's command?

a) 100,000

b) 400,000

c) 88,000

d) 48,000

Question Five

What famous phrase did Captain John Paul Jones respond with when the British navy asked if he was ready to surrender?

a) I have done all I can

b) I have not yet begun to fight

c) I must go down with my ship

d) I will sail into the sunset

Question Six

Where was the Battle of Bunker Hill actually fought?

a) In a tunnel

b) At Farnsworth Farm

c) On Breeder Hill

d) Under Bunker Bridge

Question Seven

The Continental Army's victory during the Battle of Saratoga led to which of the following?

a) Angering the British Navy

b) A complete surrender by Cornwallis

c) Convincing France to join the war

d) The death of Lafayette

Question Eight

How many times did Washington cross the Delaware River for a successful

sneak attack?

a) 3

b) 1

c) 4

d) 2

Question Nine

Who disobeyed Washington's orders at the Battle of Monmouth?

a) Benedict Arnold

b) General Lee

c) Captain John Paul Jones

d) Sgt. Pepper

Question Ten

Following his defeat at the Battle of Yorktown, what did Cornwallis hand over to French and American commanders during the formal surrender ceremony?

a) His Hat

b) His Sword

c) His Army

d) His Flag

Answers

1. **Answer:** C, John Adams

2. **Answer:** D, 8

3. **Answer:** D, 3

4. **Answer:** D, 48,00

5. **Answer:** B, I have not yet begun to fight

6. **Answer:** C, On Breeder Hill

7. **Answer:** C, Convincing France to join the war
8. **Answer:** D, 2
9. **Answer:** B, General Lee
10. **Answer:** B, His Sword

PARAGRAPH WRITING: BATTLES & THE MILITARY

Using the facts we found on the previous pages, use the 8x8 model to write your own paragraph based on the prompts below. As you write the paragraph, remember to use the foolproof formula for paragraph writing. It goes like this:

Topic Sentence (TS)
    To begin with
    For Example
    Next
    Additionally
    This clearly shows
    Finally
    Closing Sentence (CS) with a Concluding Phrase (CP)

Question Prompts

1. Choose two victories and one defeat of the Continental Army and explain how these impacted the War of Independence.

2. Although much smaller, the Continental Army used several strategies to defeat the British forces. Give two examples of these strategies and explain how they led to victory.

3. Describe the contributions of Continental Navy and how these helped lead to victory in the American Revolution.

ABOUT 8X8 PARAGRAPHS

Write Better Responses

At Middle Grade Guide we've developed easy-to-remember systems to help you do your best in school. Our Fifty Fast Facts series features not only interesting facts about history, literature, and geography but also gives you quick quizzes to reinforce your learning and sample paragraphs to help you write your own A+ short answers and essays.

Our history series is divided into the major categories or themes historians (and your teachers!) use when discussing the people, places, and events that have shaped our world. These themes are society, politics, economics, and the military. At the end of each section you'll find a multiple-choice quiz as well as a sample paragraph and several practice prompts.

Our secret weapon for acing middle school history and social studies classes is our 8x8 formula for writing paragraphs. It is made up of 8 sentences which contain at least 8 provable facts. A fact can be a name, place, date, or event, and very often you'll have two or three specific and provable facts within just once sentence. Here's an example of one sentence that contains five provable facts (very specific things you can verify were true):

Napoleon Bonaparte *was crowned the* **Emperor of France** *at a lavish ceremony at* **Notre Dame Cathedral** *in* **Paris** *on* **December 2, 1802.**

Wow. Look at that! Everything in bold is a specific, accurate, and provable fact. These are not opinions or interpretations, although you could use them to support your opinion or interpretation. There are two styles of 8x8. The first one, which you'll use most often in school, we call the *Basic 8x8*. The second one helps you to answer more complex questions, and we call it the *Advanced 8x8*. Of course, the 8x8 is just a starting point – you can include all the facts and sentences as you need to answer question prompts. We found though, that the 8x8 structure is foolproof for creating well written paragraphs that can be built into well written essays. You'll find the 8x8 structure, a sample paragraph, and more question prompts at the end of each section.

ABOUT MIDDLE GRADE GUIDE

Middle Grade Guides are written by an international team of teachers, writers, researchers, and historians. With over 30 years of experience creating textbooks, lesson plans, unit guides, and learning materials for middle grades, our team is dedicated to helping students reach their goals. Written to meet the common core competencies in the United States and Commonwealth countries, as well as Key Stage 4 in the United Kingdom. At Middle Grade Guide we know the middle years are hard - our materials make it easier.

Teachers! Get your FREE Teacher 8x8 Writing Outline here. Sign Up to receive updates on our teaching materials and textbooks.

Find us on instagram and Teachers Pay Teachers.